FINDING FAITH
— IN A —
CLOSET

SHANNON HODGE

WORKBOOK PRESS LLC
187 E Warm Springs Rd,
Suite B285, Las Vegas, NV 89119, USA

Website: https://workbookpress.com/
Hotline: 1-888-818-4856
Email: admin@workbookpress.com

Ordering Information:
Quantity sales. Special discounts are available on quantity purchases by corporations, associations, and others. For details, contact the publisher at the address above.

Library of Congress Control Number:
ISBN-13:   000-0-00000-000-0 (Paperback Version)
                000-0-00000-000-0 (Digital Version)

REV. DATE: 07/20/2022

It's in the darkness when the light of God's love shines the brightest!

Shannon Hodge

FINDING FAITH

IN A

CLOSET

"But thou, when thou prayest, enter into thy closet, and when thou hast shut thy door, pray to thy Father which is in secret, and thy Father which seeth in secret shall reward thee openly" Matthew 6:6(KJV)

Table of Contents

Acknowledgements

Dedication

All scripture passages were taken from the New King James Version unless noted otherwise.

Dedication

Finding Faith in a Closet was written first and foremost to honor and uplift the Name that is above all names, Jesus Christ, and in memory of the Most Beautiful woman in the world, my bride Angie Renaye Hodge. Angie was born May 3rd, 1970, to Jimmy and Brenda Deal. She grew up in the Sugar Loaf community of Alexander County, NC. She graduated from Alexander Central High in 1988. She went into banking right out of high school. She spent over twenty- five years in banking. Most of that time she worked in her hometown of Taylorsville. She was the town sweetheart and was dearly loved by her customers and those who knew her. She had the most vibrant smile and contagious giggle. She also had the most beautiful hazel eyes I have ever looked into. She had never met a stranger. She loved gardening and being outdoors. She had a heart for children. It was my great privilege to be able to call her my wife, even if it was but for a brief time. I am a better man today because of knowing her. She was my best friend, my helpmate, my soulmate, and the one whom my soul loves. The love we shared was so much more than a superficial love. The best way for me to describe our love is that we connected on every level, mentally, Spiritually, emotionally, and physically. But that still does not adequately put it into words. But that should not be a surprise. Our God cannot be adequately described, and it was His Love that was in our hearts. My prayer is this, if you know Jesus, I hope this book will help you to know Him more intimately. And if you do not know Him as your Savior, my hope is that you will come to know Him by the end! God bless!

Acknowledgements

I want to thank my LORD and Savior Jesus Christ for His Great Salvation! For without Him I would have no hope! I want to thank our family, friends, and both of our church families at Millersville Baptist and Little River Baptist, for all the love, prayers, and support that you have given us during this battle! I love you all! I want to thank Hav A Cup Coffee & Quality Water Service, for how you supported us and allowed me to take care of my bride during this battle. I could not have asked for a better group of people to work for and to work with! I want thank Hendrick Honda of Hickory and King Ford Lincoln of Lenoir for providing us with transportation. And I want to thank all of those who set up the fund raisers and all of those who gave. You all are a testimony of the Love of God. May the God of heaven pour out His rich blessings upon you all!

The News!

It was January 6th, 2016, and for me it started like most Wednesday mornings. The clock went off at 4 am. I got up and went to my closet where I would spend my quiet time with the LORD before getting ready for work. I would normally leave home around 6 am, to avoid school bus traffic. Before leaving I went into our bedroom to tell my bride Angie bye and to get my morning kiss. As I leaned down to kiss her, she was still sleeping, I spoke softly in her ear and told her I was leaving for work and that I loved her. That's one thing we always made sure to do! We never left each other or hung up without saying I love you. She opened her eyes looked up at me and smiled. She reached up and took me by my head and pulled me close and kissed me. She told me she loved me and for me to be careful. Like I said a typical Wednesday morning. But for my beautiful bride it was not a typical Wednesday. Even though she would be getting up shortly after I left, she had an early morning appointment to have a CT scan.

Angie had started having pain in her left side in October of 2015. She put off going to see a doctor until early November. When she went, the physician's assistant gave her a prescription for a muscle relaxer and told her to come back if her symptoms did not go away. With the holidays over and her pain getting worse, he then scheduled her to have a CT scan. I remember asking the LORD in my closet that morning to reveal what was causing her pain, but we were not prepared for the answer. CANCER!!! Stage 4 pancreatic cancer at that! It just got REAL! This was not happening to someone else! It was happening to us! On our way home I remember pounding the steering wheel in anger and yelling at God "Haven't we glorified You enough"? One thing He has shown me in my walk with Him is that He wants us to be completely honest about our feelings with Him. He already knows everything, and you're not hiding anything from Him. So, if you are angry at Him, tell Him. He's more than able to deal with your anger, disappointment, or whatever emotion you may be feeling! It has been my experience that He would not help me until I got completely honest about how I was feeling. Let me give you a little background as to why I was so angry.

Angie and I met in October of 2006. She was a personal banker at the bank where I did my banking. We went on our first date February 24th, 2007. We got married August 18th, 2007. On August 21st, 2007, Angie's only child, Bailey was killed in an ATV accident. He was only nine years old. He was full of life and very excited for Angie and I to get married. We had only been home from our honeymoon a few hours before we got the call from his father. I can still remember the long drive. The hospital where they took Bailey was about an hour away from where we live. And it is up a winding mountain road. I remember asking the Lord to get us there safely as I sped up the mountain, not knowing until we got to the hospital that Bailey was already gone. Catching my bride as she collapsed in disbelief at the news of the death of her only child is not something that I will not soon forget! You want to talk about a tough start to a marriage! But God is Faithful!

He has also shown me that everything He allows to enter our lives, is to draw us closer to Him! It does not matter if it is a blessing or a trial. It is meant to bring us into a deeper more intimate relationship and an increased dependence upon Him, not push us away! *Romans 8:28 says; "And we know all things work together for good to those who love God, to those who are the called according to His purpose."* That is a hard promise to claim in the valley of testing! But if you will claim it and believe it with all your heart, He will give you the assurance you need that good will come, even if we do not see how.

In 2008 Angie had to have a hysterectomy. When Bailey was born, there was damage to her uterus. The doctor ended up having to do procedure called endometrial ablation, where they burn the walls of the uterus to reduce menstrual flow. Early in 2008 Angie started spotting. At first, she was concerned, but that concern changed to hope. She had been praying, unbeknownst to me, for healing so that we could have a child together. But after seeing her Ob/Gyn, she told her that there was no way she could carry a child. That broke our hearts! So, she had the hysterectomy in November. But God is faithful! We were able to get involved with the youth group at our church. What a blessing!

On January 17th, 2009, my papaw Poole passed away. This was my mom's dad. He helped name me as well as helped my mom raise me the first four years of my life. I was born February 25th, 1969. My mom would not turn sixteen until that May. So, my papaw and mamaw were a big part of my life, especially in the early years of my childhood. I have never met the man who fathered me. He denied that I was his. His parents offered to adopt me to give me a "last name". But my papaw informed them that I would have a last name and it would be Poole. Back then if the father's name was placed on the birth certificate, he was held responsible for the child even if he never married the mother. His name was never placed on my birth certificate. But God is faithful! My mom kept me and a few years later the LORD brought the only man that I have ever known as daddy into our lives. He and my mom were married February 24th, 1973, one day before my fourth birthday. They have been happily married now for over forty-nine years.

After Bailey's death, Angie was not able to take the time off that she needed. She was pressured by her branch manager into coming back to work after only two weeks. But that changed in 2009. Her branch manager was replaced by a man who had been through a similar situation. He and his wife had suffered the loss of her son when he was sixteen. After he got adjusted to a new work environment and learned about our situation, he gave Angie the time off she was not able to take when the accident first happened. This was a tremendous help not only for Angie personally, but also for our marriage. It gave her time to get away from all the hassles and distractions of this life and focus on healing and her relationship with the LORD. She took advantage of this time to grow in her walk by studying the Word of God. And what a difference that made! She grew so much during that time I almost got jealous. But that was what I needed to keep me moving forward in my walk. As the spiritual leader of our home, it was my job to continue to grow in order stay in the will of God and lead my wife. I know this is not a popular view in this day and time. But God spoke in *Genesis 3:16; "To the woman He said: I will greatly multiply your sorrow and your conception; in pain you shall bring forth children; your desire shall be for you husband, and he shall rule over you."* Paul also tells us in *Ephesians 5:24 "Therefore, just as the church is subject to Christ, so let the wives be to their own husbands in everything."*

But men we have the responsibility according to God's order of things to be the Spiritual leaders of our homes, not as dictators but as shepherds. Paul also writes in *Ephesians 5:25-28 saying, "Husbands, love your wives, just as Christ also loved the church and gave Himself for her, that He might sanctify and cleanse her with the washing of water by the word, that He might present her to himself a glorious church, not having spot or wrinkle or any such thing, but that she should be holy without blemish. So, husbands ought to love their own wives as their own bodies; he who loves his wife loves himself."* So, men if your wife is not where you think she should be, examine yourself first and see if you are where you should be! If you are not living in a way that is worthy to be followed, don't get mad when no one is following!

During this time, I received a promotion. With this promotion came a significant pay increase. God is faithful! He removed financial stress from the equation while Angie was on leave. He knew that would be a hindrance to her growth. Angie had been in banking for over twenty years, and she was a numbers person. She did not need anything additional to deal with during this time of healing. But with my promotion came more responsibilities, hours, and stress. While Angie was on leave, the hours I worked were not a big issue. Working in retail management, you have anything but conventional hours. Some days you open, some days you close and some days you work in between. But when Angie went back to work, this became more and more of an issue. She worked Monday- Friday 9-5 at a bank. A typical schedule for me went like this: off Sunday, 7-5 Monday, 1-11 Tuesday, 7-5 Wednesday, off Thursday, 1-11 Friday, and 7-5 Saturday. My next week would like this: 1-11 Sunday, off Monday, 1-11 Tuesday, 7-5 Wednesday, off Thursday, 7-5 Friday, 7-5 Saturday. I would usually get one weekend off a month. Working this type of schedule started putting stress on our marriage. Angie was spending too much time at home alone. We only saw each other in passing during the week and when she was off, I was working most of the time. We did get creative with our time but that was not enough. So, in May 2010, after lots of prayer and the assurance and peace of God, we stepped out on faith, and I left my job, without any prospects or plans. But God is faithful!

The church we were attending at the time needed painting. The head of the building and grounds committee asked me if I would help with painting the church. This was one way the LORD provided. While I was painting the church, changes were taking place at the branch where Angie worked. She was getting moved against her wishes to a new position that would involve traveling from branch to branch. We did not see this as a blessing at the time. At first, we saw this as a demotion. But we could not see what God already knew. I was almost through painting the church and the job He had for me was not yet open. He used this move to help fill the gap financially between my painting the church and Him opening the door for me six months later. With the travel that was now involved with her job, Angie would be reimbursed for her mileage. Then one year and one month after leaving a good paying job, with good benefits and no prospects, just trusting in God's sovereignty and provision, He opened the door for me. The job was full time with good benefits. It was Monday- Friday, 7-3:30. I was managing the warehouse for a coffee and water delivery service that was family-owned and operated. I couldn't have asked for better people to work for or with. This was what we had been praying for and expecting. A good job with normal hours. God is faithful!

Then in November of 2011, my dad had to have thirteen inches of his colon removed. He had struggled with ulcers and diverticulitis for years. He had already had about one fourth of his stomach removed in 2005. Thankfully, everything went well with this procedure, and he is doing well today. He must closely monitor what and how much he eats but given the circumstances he is doing very well.

From 2012-2013 we were struggling emotionally at church. We were involved with the youth choir and most of the youth were in the same age range that Bailey would have been. This was making it difficult for Angie. She loved all these children dearly, but at the same time, watching them as they were growing, was a painful reminder that Bailey was no longer here. This along with other promptings from the LORD, led us to leave Angie's home church. This was not an easy decision even though we knew it was what the LORD wanted us to do. But God is faithful! He knew what was coming down the road and He knew that we would need the support of two church families. So, Angie and I spoke with our pastor at Little River and told him what we believed the LORD was leading us to do. It was difficult to leave, but at the same time there was an excitement about what the LORD was going to do in our lives.

But March 2014 started a tidal wave of storms that would change our lives and family forever. In March I was in a wreck that totaled my truck. I was sitting two cars back from a stopped school bus when, suddenly, I heard tires screeching. Before I could look in my rearview mirror, I was hit. I was hit from the back and slammed into the SUV in front of me. Fortunately, there were no major injuries.

Then on May 3, which also happens to be Angie's birthday, her dad Jimmy had a massive heart attack. It was a

Saturday morning, and we were just starting to stir around. I do not remember the exact time, but we hadn't been up long. We almost always slept in on Saturdays. It was the only day we didn't set the alarm. After calling her mom and dad, Angie and I got ready to fix breakfast. But before we could begin the phone rang and it was Angie's mom telling us to get to their house quick because something had happened to Jimmy. When we arrived, Brenda was giving Jimmy CPR in the living room floor. She continued to administer CPR as I talked with the 911 operator and tried to calm Angie, who as you can imagine, was very upset. I had called Angie's cousin Justin on the way, who at the time was an EMT, and asked him to meet us there. He along with Alexander County Rescue Squad, arrived within two minutes of our getting to the house. Jimmy was then taken to Wilkes Regional Medical Center, where he was air lifted to Wake Forest Baptist Medical Center. It turned out that one of three coronary arteries, nicknamed the "widow maker", was over ninety percent blocked. After bringing him back multiple times, they were able to do surgery and get him stabilized. But the day after getting him stabilized, he had a stroke that left him brain dead. We had to make the decision to take him off life support. After much prayer and with his family gathered around him, on May 15th, he was taken off life support and passed away shortly thereafter.

While Jimmy was in the hospital, my younger brother Matthew was admitted to Novant Medical Center, about ten minutes across town. He was diagnosed with pancreatitis. This was his second bout with the condition. He would be in and out of the hospital for the next few months before passing away on October 3rd. My brother was my best friend. Growing up we probably got into more fights because of our sister than for any other reason. But one thing that was great about our relationship is when the fight was over it was over. We let it go and moved on. We hunted and fished together, road four wheelers together, we played video games together. We always had each other's back. Matthew was a big man. Before he got sick, he was 6' 5" and weighed over three hundred and forty pounds. He was the type of man who would give you the shirt off his back. If you ever met him, you would never forget him. And speaking at his funeral is one of the most difficult things I have ever done. Now there are two more empty seats around the table, which made the holidays that much more difficult.

Angie and I have large extended families and we always make the effort to get together as a group over the holidays. God is faithful! He not only blessed us with two church families, but He also gave us one large family. When Angie and I got engaged, we didn't really include anyone in our decision to get married, not that anyone objected to us being together, but the timing was not the best in some opinions. We sat Bailey and my son Jordan down and talked with them. But there was very little discussion beyond that with anyone else in our family. There was never a doubt that the LORD had brought us together, and as far as the timing goes, He knew Bailey's time here was almost over and she was going to need the extra support and love of her soulmate. And like He does, He made the way. Angie's family loves me like one of their own and my family loved Angie the same. We would rarely refer to the others family as in-laws. It was our family. My parents became her second set of parents, as well as hers became mine. This was true for the extended family as well. That is just a God thing! He is faithful!

Then August 1, 2015, Angie's younger, and only sibling, Terry and his fiancé Jessica were in a wreck and Terry was killed. They both loved the outdoors. They had been to Doughton Park in the Blue Ridge mountains of North Carolina, to watch the sunset. They were on their way home when the driver of the car in front of them hit their brakes suddenly. Terry swerved to miss the car and over corrected. They ended up going over the side of the mountain. Jessica was able to get back up to the road and go for help, but Terry was already gone.

At this time, Angie and I had been married almost eight years. During which we had endured the passing of five people who were near and dear to our hearts. People that we had been in contact with daily for most of our lives. They were immediate family, not cousins, aunts, uncles, or even close friends. Then you add the other trials that I have not mentioned, and you have a better understanding as to why I yelled at God in anger. I have heard others say, and I'm guilty of saying it myself, you should never get angry at God, or you should never question God. I have a better understanding now as I have grown in my walk with Him. God knows all things. You are not hiding anything from Him. He already knows you are angry and hurt and disappointed. And guess what He can handle it all! The Bible is full of people who have questioned God. The greatest question in history was asked by the LORD Himself on the cross. *Matthew 27:46 says, "And about the ninth hour Jesus cried out with a loud voice, saying, "Eli, Eli, lama sabachthani?" that is "My God, My God, why have you forsaken Me?"* Angie used to think this way, until I showed her what I had been shown by the LORD. The questioning is not sin. It's when we choose not to move on from the questioning that it becomes sin. The Bible tells us in *Psalm 103:14; "For He knows our frame; He remembers that we are dust."* He knows we are going to question, because there are many things that will happen throughout our lifetime that we will not understand. God gave us free will and the ability to think logically. He also gave us our emotions. So, our questions and even our anger do not bother Him if we come

13

back to the truth about who He is. If you don't believe me read it for yourself in Jonah chapter 4.

Jonah has just finished preaching in Nineveh and a great revival took place. The whole city even the king repented in sackcloth ashes. But, instead of being happy about what God had just accomplished through him, Jonah was angry at God for sparing the Ninevites. *Jonah 4:1-4 states, "But it displeased Jonah exceedingly, and he became angry. So he prayed to the LORD and said, "Ah LORD, was not this what I said when I was still in my country? Therefore I fled previously to Tarshish; for I know that you are a gracious and merciful God, slow to anger and abundant in lovingkindness, One who relents from doing harm. Therefore now, O LORD, please take my life from me, for it is better for me to die than to live!" Then the LORD said, "Is it right for you to be angry?"* God calls David a man after His own heart. But, if you read the Psalms that David wrote, and he wrote more than half of them, you will find that David questioned God and that he freely expressed whatever emotions he was feeling at the time. The same can be said for Job. Now, I don't know if Jonah ever got over his anger, I'm sure he did. But the last thing we are told he said is in *Jonah 4:9; "Then God said to Jonah, "Is it right for you to be angry about the plant?" And he said, "It is right for me to be angry, even to death."* But Job on the other hand, in the middle of all his questions and emotions came back to this truth about God; *Job 42:1-6; "then Job answered the LORD and said: "I know that you can do everything, and that no purpose of yours can be withheld from You. You asked, 'who is this who hides counsel without knowledge?' Therefore, I have uttered what I did not understand, things too wonderful for me, which I did not know. Listen please and let me speak; You said, 'I will question you and you shall answer Me.' I have heard of You by the hearing of the ear, but now my eye sees You. Therefore, I abhor myself, and repent in ashes."* David following Job's example always brought it back to who God is and His faithfulness to His people. This is but one more example we are given to follow. God is faithful!

So, I'm pounding my steering wheel angry at God because He has allowed yet another attack come upon us! I called our pastor on the way home and gave him the news. I want you to understand before I say anything else, we love our pastor! He preaches the full counsel of the Word of God without regard. He preaches with the Love of God in his heart. Even when he steps on my toes it is seasoned with the Love of God. When he preaches, he preaches to you, not at you. But like I said, I was angry! He came to our house, and he did his best with the LORD's help to comfort and encourage us. But, for the most part, all I remember about that conversation was telling him that "I don't feel loved by God anymore"!

You see, I wasn't raised in church like Angie. My parents

had been, but they took me, my brother, and my sister out of church when we were kids. They had gotten frustrated and disheartened with the way politics and favoritism seemed to be commonplace within the churches they had attended. So, they just quit going. I am glad to say they are in church today serving the LORD. I would go to church from time to time with friends, but not on a regular basis. It took the LORD allowing one of my best friends to get killed in a car wreck, to get my attention. I had been Danny's best man when he got married in July 1990. Then in late December, just before Christmas, I got a call from his wife Lori. She told me that Danny had been killed in a car wreck and asked me if I would be one of his pall bearers. His funeral was held December 28th, 1990. As I sat two pews back from the casket, while Danny's uncle, who happens to be a Baptist preacher, was preaching the message that he had been given, something was happening to me. I went deaf. I could not hear the preacher or anyone else for that matter. All I could hear was the pounding of my heart and feeling like it was going to pound out of my chest. I had never experienced anything like that before. I knew that I had to get to the altar. The only thing I can remember praying is LORD forgive me. I knew that I had just had an encounter with the Living God. I wish that I could say that I followed Him faithfully from that point on. But I cannot!

During the next two years, I lost two jobs and my family due to divorce. I want you to understand up front, that I take full responsibility for the choices I have made in my life. I am in no way trying place the fault at my parents' feet. They gave me their best advice! I chose to ignore them. I thought I knew better than they. Turns out I was wrong. But since I was not raised in church and I did not have the Bible as my foundation, I had no idea how to lean on the Lord during the storms of life. I cannot remember ever hearing my parents pray or seeing them read their Bibles. Without realizing it, the message they were sending was, God is not important. You will just have to do the best you can. Well, the best that I could do, led me down the road to alcohol and drug abuse. I was hurting, and I was angry, and I just walked away. I walked away from the Only One who could have helped me. I lived a prodigal life until May 2006.

Then as I lie flat on my back, on my back porch, after my second wife had left, because of the anger issues I had at the time. I looked up to the sky and said "It's ALL Yours' LORD. I don't want it anymore!" I didn't want the anger, the bitterness, the unforgiveness, the drugs or the alcohol! I surrendered it ALL! EVERYTHING and EVERYONE in my life was His! The day of salvation and the day of total surrender do not always take place at the same time. The LORD saved me on

December 28th, 1990, but I did not fully surrender to Him until May of 2006. The past twelve plus years, have been the MOST DIFFICULT time of my life! But they have also been the MOST REWARDING! God is faithful!

After our pastor prayed with us and left, I started researching trying to get an understanding of this new enemy. At the same time, I began going deeper in the Word of God. I wanted a greater understanding of the love of God. *Jeremiah 29:11-14 says, "For I know the thoughts I think toward you, says the LORD, thoughts of peace and not of evil, to give you a future and a hope. Then you will call upon Me and go and pray to Me, and I will listen to you. And you will seek Me and find Me, when you search for Me with all your heart. I will be found by you says the LORD and I will bring you back from your captivity."* One of our prayers during this battle was, "LORD don't let us miss You! Open our eyes to see You move!" I can say without hesitation, He has answered that prayer in many ways. God is Faithful! I have a greater understanding of the love of God now, than at any time in my walk with Him! Somethings we can only learn in the valleys of this life!

The Need Supplied

Our first appointment was with a surgeon at the cancer center at Wake Forest Baptist Hospital. During the initial consultation the doctor commented that the type of cancer Angie had was usually seen in much older patients and seemed genuinely puzzled that they were seeing this type of cancer occurring in much younger people. When I commented that our diets were a contributing factor, he said "maybe". After another scan, he determined that surgery was not an option, because the main tumor was wrapped around an artery and the cancer had spread to her liver. He sent us to an oncologist to set up treatments. During our only meeting with the oncologist, I asked her what type of diet Angie needed to be on, and she said some sort of high protein diet she supposed. I also asked her about using natural cancer fighters and immune boosters during her treatments and she commented that she did not know what they would do to her and that they could kill her. After meeting with this doctor, I knew we needed to look for other options. So, we went home, and I continued my researching.

The Bible says in *Genesis 2:7, "And the Lord God formed man out of the dust of the ground, and breathed into his nostrils the breath of life; and man became a living being."* This passage tells us that our bodies are organic in nature. This should also tell us that we should be mindful about what we put in them. Being organic in nature, our bodies are not designed to ingest and process the onslaught of artificial chemical additives in our foods. Add to these refined sugars, GMOs, any unhealthy habits such as alcohol or recreational drugs, and lastly if you regularly take any prescription or OTC medications, you have a recipe for all types of disease not just cancer.

I grew up playing sports and working out. My parents got me my first weight bench and weight set when I was in seventh or eighth grade. My favorite sport to play and coach was football. The Good LORD created me to be an athlete and if it were not for bad decisions on my part, I would be coaching football or training athletes in some form or fashion today. So, taking care of my body is nothing new to me. For as long as I can remember I have looked at food as fuel and my body as a car. My thoughts are if you put good stuff in it, you will perform better, you will have more energy and feel better overall as your body functions more efficiently. If you put bad stuff in it, it eventually catches up with you, because you have less energy, feel worse overall and your body begins to break down more rapidly and function less efficiently. So, one of the most important requirements for me was a place that took a holistic approach to treatment, not just chemo and radiation, but a body, mind, and spirit approach.

When I began my research for other treatment facilities, I came across the Cancer Treatment Centers of America. I started a chat with a very nice lady on the website. She then called and started explaining to us what all the center had to offer. Their focus is not just on fighting the cancer. They take a more holistic approach by integrating dietary and nutritional supplementation along with chemo and/or radiation. They also offer additional therapies such as acupuncture, massage, chiropractic treatments to help alleviate stress and promote a healing response. We talked for a few minutes. She then turned me over to a gentleman named Matt, who helped with scheduling. He also helped to make sure we got to the right center, as each center specializes in certain types of cancer. The best option for Angie was in Newnan, GA, three hundred twenty-one miles away from our home in Taylorsville, NC. He explained to us that we would come to the center. They would do an evaluation process that included blood work and various scans and then determine a course of action designed specifically for Angie. He explained this process usually takes three to five days. After he finished telling us how the trips usually go, we had to explain our situation to him. Our situation went like this.

We have a 75 lb. pit bull name Leilu. She is her mama's baby, and she cannot be kenneled, because the vet's office is afraid of her. That is another story altogether. The only person she would let stay in the house with her is Angie's mom. Well, Angie is not going all the way to Georgia without her mom. As I was explaining this to Matt, Angie's friend DeAnna called her cell phone to check one her. She also told her about the outing that some of the branch managers had earlier that day. She told her that the first thing they did was get together and lift us up in prayer. She said they asked the LORD to give us direction and make a way for us to go to CTCA. Then Angie told her that I was on the phone with Matt from CTCA. That is just a God thing! He is faithful!

Matt had put me on a brief hold while he worked to come up with a solution for our situation. When he came back, he told us that one of the hotels they shuttle to is pet friendly. So, we could bring Angie's mom, Brenda, and our pit baby Leilu. All we had to do now was get a way to the center. Neither vehicle we owned would carry everything we would need to carry with us. Angie told DeAnna that we were going to be able to go, but we needed something bigger to drive. She told Angie not to worry. She had that covered. God is faithful! *Philippians 4:19 states; "And my God shall supply all your need according to His riches in glory by Christ Jesus."* DeAnna called

Angie back a few minutes later. She has a friend who is a sales manager at a car dealership. They supplied us with a new van to drive. All we had to pay for was the gas for the trip. But this was just one of many ways God provided for us during this battle. He was moving, and we had front row seats. From that moment forward I knew that it was in His hands, and I believed with all my heart that we were going to be part of a miracle. This was Him working in my heart.

By this time, it had been about a month since the diagnosis. I was not happy about the situation, but I was no longer angry at God for allowing the cancer. The whole time I am researching pancreatic cancer, I am staying in The Word, searching Him out. I do not remember the exact day, but I do remember the revelation that He gave me that morning in my closet. I had had a conversation a few months prior with a friend of mine from work. He happens to be an atheist. I am thankful that the LORD has made a way for our paths to cross. We were talking and sharing our beliefs with one another. At the end of our conversation, he made the comment that if there is a God, He made a mistake when He created Satan, and that sin was a result of His mistake. I am ashamed to say that at that moment I didn't have a counter to that opinion. I just left it at your missing the point it's His plan, not ours. He can do what He chooses because He is God!

But, on this morning as I entered my closet, I was angry, not at God, but at Satan, and I asked God directly, "Why did you create him in the first place knowing all the trouble he would cause?" I am not going say I heard God's audible voice. But what I did hear came from Him straight to my heart. He said "So, that you would know that I love you." At first, that was a hard pill to swallow. I must admit I was a bit confused. But, as I sat in dark silence, He began to open my understanding. The Bible says in *I John 4:8; "He who does not love, does not know God, for God is love."* The Bible also says in *Hebrews 13:8; "Jesus Christ is the same yesterday, today, and forever."* If God is love and never changes, why is it that Adam and Eve did not understand the unconditional sacrificial love of God? Because the Bible tells us the plan of salvation has always been the cross. There was never another plan. *I Peter 1:18-20 says, "knowing that you were not redeemed with corruptible things, like silver or gold, from your aimless conduct received by tradition of your fathers, but with the precious blood of Christ, as of a lamb without blemish and without spot. He indeed was foreordained before the foundation of the world, but was manifest in these last times for you."* In other words, God knew that Adam and Eve would disobey Him before He ever created anything. And knowing this He still created them.

Adam and Eve had something no one else in history

has had. They walked daily with the LORD in the Garden of Eden, and yet still did not understand how much they were loved by Him. Why is that? It is because they knew nothing else but His love. To put it another way. There had not been any troubles, hardship, or sin. Because everything was perfect! Just as God created it to be. Enter Satan, Jesus tells us in *John 8:44; "You are of your father the devil, and the desires of your father you want to do. He was a murderer from the beginning, and does not stand in the truth, because there is no truth in him. When he speaks a lie, he speaks from his own resources, for he is a liar and the father of it."* One reason Satan hates mankind is because we are created in the image of God, which cannot be said about any other created thing. He also hates us because God loves us! So, Satan's desire is to destroy anyone and everyone he can, especially those who have placed their faith in Jesus as Lord and Savior. *I Peter 5:8 says, "Be sober, be vigilant; because your adversary the devil walks about like a roaring lion, seeking whom he may devour."* So, he comes to the garden possessing the body of a serpent and tempts Eve.

Just a side note and something for you to think about, the serpent in its original form was not a snake. Make no mistake it was reptilian in form, but it was not a snake that deceived Eve. A closer reading of the passage makes this very clear, *Genesis 3:1 says, "Now the serpent was more cunning than any beast of the field which the LORD God had made. And he said to the woman, "Has God indeed said, 'You shall not eat of every tree of the garden?"* Did you catch that, *"beast of the field"* part? Beasts of the field have legs. Also, how can it be a curse if he is already crawling on his belly when God curses him in verse fourteen when He says, *"Because you have done this, you are cursed more than all cattle, and more than every beast of the field; on your belly you shall go, and you shall eat dust all the days of your life," Genesis 3:14.* So all of the depictions of a snake in a tree deceiving Eve are incorrect in their interpretation of the passage. The question that must then be asked is this a deliberate deception? Why keep the original form hidden?

Satan knew that if he could get Eve, he would get Adam, because he knew that Adam would not turn away from his wife. There is an old saying; "You don't know what you have until it's gone." Well, that is what happened. Adam and Eve got what they thought they wanted, which was the knowledge of good and evil so they could be like God. But lost what they already had, which was an intimate personal relationship with God, their Creator. And after they were driven out of paradise, they longed more for what they lost instead of rejoicing over what they thought they gained.

But that is what it took. There must be contrast. You cannot understand courage, without fear. You cannot understand joy without sorrow. The same applies to love. We lose so much of the meaning in translation from Greek to English and even more from Hebrew to English. In the Greek language there are four words that describe four different types of love, phileo (friendship), storge(family), eros (sexual), and agape (unconditional). The first three are types of conditional love that do not require the presence of sin or evil to be understood. But without the presence of sin or evil we would never be able to understand unconditional love. Unlovable conditions must exist to understand unconditional love. If all you have ever known is love, how do you truly know what love is? Love is not just some feel good emotion. It is a choice that involves much more than emotion. When He gave this understanding to me, it completely changed how I looked at the battle ahead of us. It also took me to a deeper understanding of how much He really loves us!

People have been asking this question for centuries. Why are we here? Well, I'm going to answer it, at least in part. Are you ready for it? The answer is love. God gave us our emotions. Which means he has the same emotions that He gave us. Because He cannot give us something that He Himself does not possess. There is not a man, woman, or child that does not want to be loved and to have someone to love. If we have that desire, where do you think it came from. Exactly, it came from God. Which is why He created us. He created it all out of His desire to love us and be loved by us. He will not force His love on anyone and will not demand that anyone love Him. That is why He gave us free will! He does not want a bunch of robots or yes men. He wants us to willingly give our hearts to Him. That is one reason it grieved his heart when Adam and Eve fell for the lies of Satan. He knew what they did not at the time. Satan played on their pride. He told them they would be like God, knowing the difference between good and evil. But what he did not tell them was, that they would lose the intimate fellowship that they already had with God, because of their direct disobedience.

With this new understanding, we were determined to follow the LORDS' leading and fight this new enemy without fear. Our first trip to CTCA was excruciatingly long. The directions to the center are easy enough. Take I-85S all the way to exit 47, in Newnan GA. The center is less than a mile from the exit. You turn right onto Bullsboro Dr. and then turn left at the first light onto Celebrate Life Parkway. But what time you hit the outskirts of Atlanta, will determine the length of the trip. We hit Atlanta at the worst part of the day, around 4pm. It took us over three hours to drive the last seventy miles. The total travel time was just over ten hours. It was after seven when we arrived at the hotel. We all were exhausted. We checked in and then just tried to get some rest. Neither one of us was that fond of driving or riding. When we would go on vacation, if we were going more than a couple of hours away, we made plans to stay at least five days. We were not the types that would jump in the car on Friday after work and drive to the beach, which is at least five hours away from us, and turn around and come back Sunday. So, it was a great relief to finally get off the road.

The next morning, we started the evaluation process, which took three days. At the end of the evaluation, her team of doctors brought us the plan and we were ready to start treatments. Before she could start however, Angie ended up at the centers' urgent care. She had an allergic reaction to the pain patch that she had been given. Angie was hypersensitive to medications. One reason was her size. She wasn't quite five feet tall, even though she would tell you different. Bailey would pick at her and tell her, and others, that she wasn't but three feet tall. On a good day he would say she was four feet tall. And she weighed 113 lbs. So, this delayed her port placement and the start of her treatment by another day.

By this time, we had been at the center for six days, and Leilu, our pit baby, was getting adjusted to her new surroundings. She thought the whole hotel was her territory. So, whenever I would take her out for a walk, I tried to make sure there wasn't anyone out in the hall. Because if there was, she would let them have it. I couldn't tell you how many of the house keepers she scared. In case you don't know anything about pits, they are extremely territorial and extremely protective of their owners. They're AWESOME dogs, with an undeserved reputation because of people who raise them to fight. Even though she was getting adjusted, we all were ready to get back home.

Since Angie's reaction to the pain patch delayed the start of her port placement, the doctor scheduled it and her first treatment on the same day. But that proved to be too much! After having her port placed, she had just a few hours before the start of her first treatment. When we got to infusion, she was put in room six. They started her pre-meds and after that, her first chemo drug. She did fine, until they started her next chemo drug. She started to have an allergic reaction and they stopped her treatment. So, by now we have been here for more than a week and must back up and punt. After a couple of more days, when Angie was able to travel, we went back home. We started praying and asked everyone to pray with us for guidance for us and her doctors. On our next trip, two weeks later, the LORD answered that prayer.

The Next Step

We made the decision to fly on our next trip to CTCA. Our thinking was it would be faster. The center provides valet service for those who choose to fly, so you are not confined to a hotel room or rent a car to get around. But, by the time we got to airport and boarded the plane, landed, and then waited for the valet from CTCA to pick us up and take us to the hotel. We discovered that flying was not any quicker than driving. Only now, we were in Newnan dependent on the valet and shuttle service to get around. From that point on we decided to drive. Which that suited Angie just fine. She did not like to fly at all! She hated flying more than riding!

When we got to the hotel, we got settled in, and decided to go down to the patio and relax. That is when the LORD answered our prayer for direction. There was another couple Jim and Karen, sitting outside by one of the gas fireplaces. We went over and sat down and started a conversation. They were from Pennsylvania. They were here for Jim's prostate cancer. Angie and Karen, hit it off very well. But that was nothing new for Angie. She had never met a stranger. She did her best to let her light shine before others. That is one of the many reasons her customers ADORED her! Karen was telling Angie about the research that she had been doing. Then she asked which of us was the patient. Angie told her; she was. Karen then asked her what type? She told her stage 4 pancreatic. Karen then looked at me and asked if I had heard about Abraxane? I told her, I had not, but I would look it up. She told us that it had been designed specifically for pancreatic cancer. God is faithful! He had that couple there for that specific purpose. When we went back to the room, I looked up Abraxane to double check what Karen had told me. The next morning at Angie's appointment, I asked her doctor what he knew about Abraxane. He promptly asked me what I knew about it. I told him that all I knew was, that it is a chemo drug designed for pancreatic cancer. He then told us that he was considering switching Angie to that treatment. He then discussed the differences between the treatments. And that's when we decided to go with Abraxane. This time when we get up to infusion, Angie was put in room 35. They got her premeds in her and then started the chemo. Thankfully, no allergic reactions! God is faithful! Another of many answered prayers.

When she was finished, we went back to the room to rest and start packing. We were supposed to fly out the next morning. But as the day went on, I knew that there was no way Angie would be able to fly. She was just too weak to go through the whole process again. By this time all the car rental lots had closed. There was one however, that would open at

12 noon, the next day, which was a Sunday. So, that was our plan. We would call the rental company the next day and head home then. But that was not God's plan. DeAnna called to check on Angie. Angie told her what we had planned to do since she was not able to fly. DeAnna told her to sit tight, and she would call her back. A few minutes later she called back, DeAnna and her husband Chad borrowed a van from another couple that we go to church with. Chris and Renee were at their house visiting. This allowed them to take Chad and DeAnna's children, BreAnna and Cole with them. They stopped what they were doing to drive all the way to Newnan, GA, to pick us up. That is the love of God at work in the hearts of His people. They got to the hotel between 1am-2am Sunday morning, and we headed back home. That is also the sovereign hand of God at work!

In the Bible, numbers have certain meanings. For instance, Angie's first treatment was in room six. In the Bible, six is the number for man. That first treatment was the doctors' choice, and it went bad. The number thirty-five in the Bible is the number for hope. This was God's choice! He orchestrated ALL of that. Even though she was not able to fly, she did not have an allergic reaction. That was just one example of many times He answered prayers for direction and provision.

Another example, until the middle of July 2016 we were

provided vehicles to drive. There were two different dealerships that loaned us vehicles. And a dear couple from our church Randall and Lisa, let us drive their van on many of our trips. But in July the LORD provided, us with opportunity to trade for a larger SUV. But this was not an easy decision for Angie to make. Angie drove a white Nissan Juke. She loved this little car. And it suited her to a tee. Her name was Grace. Angie named her vehicles. But Grace was not the most comfortable of rides. Especially for long trips and it lacked the size needed to carry everything we needed to carry with us on our trips to the center. When we were dating, Angie had a 1999 Lexus 300. Her name was Lexi. Lexi was the vehicle, she had for a big part of Bailey's life. She drove Lexi until July 2013. That's when we decided it was time to trade. It was going to cost more than what we wanted to pay, to do the engine work that needed to be done. She fell in love with the Jukes' body style, and we found one online and went and test drove it. That's all it took. She was hooked. It was a bittersweet moment for her when we traded Lexi for Grace. And that's why she named her Grace. Because it's ALL about God's AMAZING GRACE!

But then July rolled around, and the insurance company settled the claim from the wreck that I had been in, in 2014. This made it possible to trade Grace. My car was paid for, and we did not need take on another car payment at this time. So,

I told Angie to make sure she found what she wanted. That's when she found Hope. Hope is a 2015 Nissan Rogue. She is Dark Green with beige interior and a panoramic sunroof. The same dealership that had loaned us the vans had Hope. But she was on another lot. They brought her to the Hickory location closest to us, and we traded Grace. Angie liked Hope, but she did not love her like she did Grace.

Now that we had the direction, we had asked for concerning treatment regimen, we turned our focus to doing our part. Another thing He has shown me in my walk with Him, is this, He will not do our part for us. When He shows you something that you need to do, do it! Because He is not going to do it for you and if you are disobedient, you can hinder His hand. Especially when it comes to healing. *James 5:14-16 says, "Is there any among you sick? Let him call for the elders of the church, and let them pray over him, anointing his head with oil in the name of the LORD. And the prayer of faith will save the sick and the LORD will raise him up. And if he has committed sins, he will be forgiven. Confess your trespasses to one another and pray for one another that you may be healed. The effective fervent prayer of a righteous man avails much." I Corinthians 6:19-20 also says, "Or do you not know that your body is the temple of the Holy Spirit who is in you, whom you have from God, and you are not you own? For you were bought with a price; therefore glorify*

God in your body and in your spirit which are God's." I've heard Charles Stanley say many times, "Be obedient to the LORD and leave the consequences to Him."

This applies to every area of our lives! Including what we put into our bodies! There are so many people in this country that take their health for granted and the big pharmaceutical companies are making billions because of it. People think they can put whatever they want to in their bodies without any consequences. Well, they are wrong! You get to make the choices about what you put in your body. But you DO NOT I repeat you DO NOT get to choose the consequences of those choices! One of the basic principles in the Bible and in life is this, you reap what you sow, more than you sow, later than you sow. The Bible says in *Galatians 6:7-9; "Do not be deceived God is not mocked; for whatever a man sows, that he will also reap. For he who sows to his flesh will of the flesh reap corruption, but he who sows to the Spirit will of the Spirit reap everlasting life. And let us not grow weary while doing good, for in due season we shall reap if we do not lose heart."* A great percentage of the diseases and sickness in this country are a result of people who do not believe in this principle. We think we know better than the One who created us in His image. By the way, how is that working out? Each year there are millions of new cases of cancer and millions more deaths. The only people who prosper in sickness are drug companies and medical professionals. Cancer alone generates over $100 billion a year to big pharma. If people would start being intentional about their health, we could take a huge chunk of that money away from big pharma. But there is a general lack of understanding this basic principle and plain rebellion. Some people just do not care. They are going to do what they want regardless. Some people just do not understand the connection between diet and overall health.

That is the group that Angie fell into. She truly did not understand the importance of her diet. Especially now, with her diagnosis. That was another reason for choosing CTCA. Her team included a naturopath and a dietician. They had the knowledge of how to treat the body through diet and supplementation. The LORD used these two ladies to help us make better choices of what to eat and how to prepare foods to get the most nutritional support. Along with the different supplements that help to keep the immune system built up and those that fight cancer. Do not ever let a doctor tell you that there are no natural cancer fighters, because that is a LIE! This was our part. The LORD showed us what to do. Now it was our time to be obedient.

Another thing the LORD has made abundantly clear during this battle is, if sin contributed to your sickness, do not expect God to heal you if you are not willing to repent of that sin. Example, if you have diabetes, and it is because you choose not to eat the way you should if you refuse repent of that attitude do not expect to be healed. If you have cancer that smoking contributed to, do not expect healing if you are not willing to repent even if you are not able to stop immediately. If you have alcohol induced cirrhosis and you refuse to repent, do not expect God to heal you. When you refuse to repent you put hand cuffs on God. Again, I say, when He shows you what to do, do it! This does not mean He will heal you. But it does mean that you have removed all barriers that would keep Him from healing you. Repentance is not just quitting something or adding something. That is all well and good. But genuine repentance comes from the heart. It is the act of agreeing with God about sin and turning around and going in the opposite direction. He cannot and will not condone sin in a believer's life! And He will not reward those who refuse to repent. God looks at sin different than we do. All sin is offensive to Him. But we tend to think a bit too highly of ourselves and think that some "little sins" are ok. One of those little sins is how we take care of our bodies. Remember what *I Corinthians 6:20 says, "For you were bought at a price, therefore glorify God in your body and in your spirit, which are God's."* He has given us one body and one life. Like I said before if you are not willing to repent do not expect His healing. That would go against His nature. He will not reward an unrepentant heart. That would be Him condoning sin and He is not going to do that. Sin is the very reason He sent His Son Jesus to die on the cross. He died for ALL our sins! Even our so called "little sins"!

With the direction of Angie's naturopath and dietician, we started changing our diets and how we prepared food. This was the most difficult part for Angie in the beginning. She had never focused on her diet. Different people look at food in different ways. Like I said before, I look at food as fuel. I grew up playing sports. My uncle Gary, my mom's younger brother, was ten when I was born and he had me dribbling a basketball by the time I was two years old. I have spent most of my life involved with sports and working out. Growing up I can never remember looking at food any other way. I still look at it that way today. Do not get me wrong, I love good food. I just look at it from a different point of view. But for Angie, it was a different story. We used to watch cooking shows together and they would talk about comfort foods. Well, I had no idea what they were talking about. But Angie did. That's how she looked at food. Because she grew up in a family that put a lot of focus on getting together around the table sharing meals. And not just around the holidays. Her aunts, uncles and cousins stayed close to the family home. They would get together at her nanas' house on Sundays after church and have a meal on a regular basis. These meals became known as "happy meals".

This continued until her nana went home to be with the LORD in 2005. We still have the "happy meals" today, just not as often.

So, for Angie, food was a big part of her life growing up, and she looked at it from a different point of view than I did. I remember telling her from the beginning, that this battle would not be just physical and emotional. It was a spiritual battle also. The flesh does not like change! Especially when it requires taking something away from it. It wants what it wants, and it will not give in without a fight. The Bible says in *Galatians 5:17; "For the flesh lusts against the Spirit, and the Spirit against the flesh; and these are contrary one to another so that you do not do the things that you wish."* Angie grew up on a typical southern diet with lots of carbs and fried foods. This type of diet will not help you defeat cancer. She needed to give up all starches like white breads, pastas, rice, sugar, and potatoes. She was going to need to limit red meat and pork to sixteen ounces a week combined not each. She was going to need to eat more fish, chicken, and turkey and a greater variety of vegetables, especially green vegetables. These were very big changes that we needed to make, to give her the nutrition that her body was going to need to stay strong during our battle. I say our battle because cancer invades every area of your home and life! You are constantly aware that there is an enemy inside you, and its' only mission is to kill you! That's why you must be even more aggressive in your battle strategy. I was continually doing research, looking for anything that we needed to add or take away. One principle in life that applies to everything, no matter what it is, whether it is animal, vegetable, or microscopic organisms is if you take away its' food supply, it will die. Nothing, not even cancer can survive if you take away its' food source. But this is not as easy as it sounds. Especially, for someone who finds comfort in certain types of foods that are known to feed cancer. This is where we had our biggest differences of opinion.

Like I said before, I grew up playing sports, and football was my favorite. It was my favorite from the very first time I put on pads at the age of nine. One reason I enjoyed it so much was because you got to hit people without getting in trouble. In my mind what nine-year-old boy wouldn't enjoy that. I played both offense and defense, but defense was my favorite. I played with an aggressive, attacking mentality and that is the way I looked at this cancer. It was trying to take the life of my Best Friend, who also happened to be my Beautiful Bride! In my mind I wanted to hit this cancer as hard as we could. That meant, she needed to quit smoking immediately and we needed to make the dietary changes all at once. My plan was to choke off its' food supply from the very start and shock her body. But she could not make herself give it all up at once. She said she would not make it if she did. That is where the battle becomes spiritual. She wanted to cut back gradually, instead of all at once. In her mind, she had already given up so much and had endured so many losses, and this was an area of her life, she was not ready to fully surrender. So, I gave way, and we cut back gradually. I didn't like it but, adding stress and frustration to the situation would only make things worse. So, I really tried not to fuss. But I reminded her as lovingly as I could on a regular basis about making the changes.

We went through the first six treatments, making the trip every two weeks. Then it was time for her PET scan. When we got the results, they were not what we were wanting. The scan showed that the cancer had progressed. The labs showed no change in the tumor markers. Her doctor came to us about going to a different treatment. Looking back now, if I had it to do over again, I wouldn't have agreed to the change. But, at that time, we were listening to a doctor who has been dealing with this type of cancer for years. We were trusting in his judgement and experience. So, we agreed to the change. This treatment regimen was so much more difficult on Angie than the first. With her first regimen, we were usually at the center for 1-2 nights. We would go down the day before her appointments and depending on what time she got out of infusion, we would either head back that evening or the following morning. With this new regimen we were there 3-4 nights. So, it was not just the new treatment, it was the stress of being away from home longer. During this round of treatments, we would try to make the most of our trips. We would go to the movies, go out to eat, or go shopping. Which she loved to do. But it is hard to fully enjoy that time together when one of you has a bag with a chemo pump, pumping poison into their body for forty-six straight hours and the other tries to stay positive all the while I am seeing this taking such a toll on someone that I love with all my heart!

Love, no one truly knows what love is or how to love, until they have surrendered to the LORD Jesus. I say that speaking from my own experience. Before we met in 2006 and married in 2007, Angie and I both had been married previously, myself twice. If we had been surrendered to the Lord when we were younger, most likely none of those marriages would have taken place. But we were not, and they did. But, in 2006, before we ever met, we both surrendered our hearts and lives to the lordship of Jesus Christ. When He fills your heart with His love, it takes on a whole new perspective. It becomes less about you and more about them! Less about what I can get and how it benefits me and more about how I can give and put a smile on their face. That is the difference Christ makes in the human heart. And that is what we tried to let the world see. When people saw us, they saw two imperfect people doing their best to live in surrender to the will of a perfect, holy, almighty God. We were not perfect in any sense of the meaning, but we were perfect for each other. When the Lord brought us together, it was like we had known each other all our lives. So much so, that we tried to figure out where we could have met, had we made different choices in our past. What we figured out was, that we probably would have met at a community college that was located between us. I graduated from Starmount High in 1987. I enrolled at Wilkes Community College in the fall of 1987. Angie graduated from Alexander Central High 1988. She planned to enroll at WCC in the fall of 1988. We do not know who made the decision not to go first. But neither of us enrolled in the fall of '88. Only the Good LORD knows what would have come about had we made the choice to enroll that fall. I can honestly say, without meaning any disrespect to either of my ex-wives or anyone else I dated prior, Angie was my first true love!

If there had been any way for me to take the cancer from her or take the treatments for her, I would have gladly! I am the type of person who wants to fix things and make things better. But that was not an option here. This treatment regimen made her so sick and all I could do was watch and pray. I had never felt so helpless! I don't remember the date, but I do remember it was during this round of treatments that the LORD sent by *Psalm 46:10, "Be still and know that I am God; I will be exalted among the nations, I will be exalted in the earth!"* That is what He does! He sends His children what they need when they need it! His timing is always perfect! Whether it was a verse of scripture or words of encouragement from family, friends, or other patients, we always got what we needed when we needed it. God is faithful!

Thankfully, we got through that round of treatments without too many issues. But they took their toll on my bride mentally, physically, and emotionally. Angie had the most beautiful spirit about her. I may be partial, but that's ok, it's my opinion. She was the most beautiful woman I have ever known. She not only had outer beauty, but she also had inner beauty. She had totally surrendered her life to the Lord, and it showed. She had never met a stranger. Angie was outgoing, optimistic, and always smiling. She was full of life even after the battles we had already been though including the first round of treatments. But, by the end of the second round, she was so exhausted and felt so bad, that we decided that no matter what the results of the next scan were, we were going back to the first regimen. When we got the results, the cancer had progressed and there was no change in her tumor markers. We are now in September and getting ready to start her third round of six treatments. It would have been easy to get discouraged, but with all that we had witnessed the LORD doing plus going back to her previous treatment regimen we remained positive. The LORD also gave us during this time *Ephesians 3:20, "Now to Him who is able to do exceedingly, abundantly above all that we ask or think, according to the power that works in us."* So, we started this third round, with a renewed sense of hope.

The Understanding

Up to this point, Angie was able to manage her pain with OTC pain relievers. But that changed in the middle of October. She had to start taking low dose oxycontin and a low dose time release morphine. This was something that we did not want her to have to do, but she did not have much of a choice. Before she started her second round of treatment, Angie's doctor suggested that she have a pain block. After we talked it over and prayed about it, she decided not to have it at that time. She didn't want to go through another procedure if she didn't have to. We were still trusting and believing she was going to beat this. But, with her pain increasing on top of the side effects of the pain meds, we decided that it would be best for her to go ahead and have the procedure. We got the next available appointment, which would be two weeks later our next trip down. She would have her pain block first and then she was to have her treatment the next day. Angie was nervous about having this procedure. But since we had to stay in the center on this trip, we couldn't bring Leilu. That also meant Angie's mom, who would stay with her at our house during our trips, could not come, because Brenda was the only one who could stay with Leilu. So, Angie's uncle Hal and her cousin April, drove to the center to be there for her procedure. That is another expression of God's love, during this battle. When the procedure was finished, we visited with them for a little bit before they turned right around and headed back home.

Before she started this round of treatments, Angie made a much stronger commitment to eliminating foods from her diet that helped to feed her cancer. Don't take that the wrong way. She had made a bunch of changes already. But there was still room for improvement. As I am writing this, I have wondered if that is not the reason for the increased pain level. Angie was depriving the cancer of its' food supply along with mounting an attack against it with supplements, diet, and chemo. We were not expecting any good news from her labs on this trip to the center, especially with her pain level elevated. But we were caught totally off guard when we got her lab results. This whole time during her treatments, we have been monitoring two different tumor markers, CA 19-9, and CEA. From the very beginning the CA 19-9 was above 20,000 units which was as high as the center could measure. The CEA had gotten above 7. The CA 19-9 dropped for the first time, to a level where we could get a reading. It dropped down to 17,700 units. This is the first time during the treatment process that it was able to be counted. The CEA dropped to a little above 5. Talk about elated! That is what we had been waiting for! Things were heading in the right direction. Now all she had to do, was get her pain block and have her treatment the next day and we would be home resting later that night. At least that is how we had it planned. But that is not what happened. She had the pain block as planned. The procedure went well. It eliminated 95% of her pain, allowing Angie to quit taking the narcotics that made her feel so bad.

But later that evening, she started having diarrhea. She was up and down all night. I ended up taking her to the urgent care in the center. They did her labs and took samples and when all was said and done, she had a bowel infection called C. diff. They gave her fluids and antibiotics. We went from being on top of the mountain to back down in the valley. Angie could not have her treatment. She would be on these antibiotics for two weeks. This is going to push her to a minimum of five weeks without treatments. This was not the news we wanted to hear. Especially now that we had the evidence that everything, we had been doing at home was starting to work. Most of that stopped as well, after she started taking the antibiotics. They were so strong and made her so sick that she could not keep anything down. One of the main side effects was nausea and vomiting. During the two weeks of antibiotics, Angie went from 107 lbs. to 92 lbs. Prior to getting C diff, if Angie was wearing her wig, you would have never known she had cancer. She was taking her mom to the grocery store. We were able to go to church. She was active around the house. It would normally take her about four days to start getting her energy back after a treatment, but then she was good to go. Her immune system was not strong enough to work in the public daily, but like I said if she had her wig on you could not tell she was sick. But losing all the weight that she did, took a toll on her. She was tired, and it was starting to show in her eyes. I could see it and I tried to not to let it show on my face. We refused to give in to the fears and doubts that the enemy was hurling at us. We made the choice to trust in the One who is able, despite the circumstances. We were still expecting her to beat this cancer.

The next two months were the most difficult time of testing I had ever endured. It ended up being six weeks between her treatments. When we arrived at the center for her appointment, her labs were not as bad as I was expecting, but they were worse than what they had been prior to the infection, and both markers went back up and never came back down. The LORD again sent by what we needed, when He gave us *Psalm 91:14-16; "Because he has set his love upon Me, therefore I will deliver him; I will set him on high, because he has known My name. He shall call upon Me, and I will answer him; I will be with him in trouble; I will deliver him and honor him. With long life I will satisfy him and show him My salvation."* Man, talk about encouragement. This is the LORD speaking to one of His children. We took these verses and personalized them. What I mean by that is this, we put our names in every place that had a personal pronoun that does not apply to the LORD. So, for me it read like this; "Because Shannon has set his love on Me, therefore I will deliver Shannon; I will set Shannon on high, because Shannon has known My name. Shannon shall call upon Me, and I will answer Shannon; I will be with Shannon in trouble; I will deliver Shannon and honor Shannon. With long life I will satisfy Shannon and show Shannon My salvation." This was a great help and encouragement to us at the time. But Angie was never able to regain her appetite or gain any of the weight back. Then on January 25th, 2017, with our family and close personal friends around her, my Beautiful Bride, my best friend, the one whom my soul loves, went home to be with the LORD.

Watching her lose this battle was very difficult for me to swallow. After all that we had seen the LORD do during this time. I believed with all my heart that, Angie was going to come out of this battle victorious and that we were going to have the rest of our lives to spend together, while we waited for the LORD's return. I remember sometime after Bailey was killed; Angie mentioned that we needed to purchase our burial plots. I told her that we were not going to need them. I honestly believed that we were going to go together when the rapture of the church takes place. But that was my plan, not the Lord's. I don't know why He allowed Angie to get cancer in the first place. I don't know why he allowed her to be taken. Part of the reason may be because He wanted me to write this book. The Bible tells us in *Ephesians 2:10; "For we are His workmanship, created in Christ Jesus unto good works, which God has prepared beforehand that we should walk in them."* He has specific works for us to do while we are on this earth. I honestly cannot say that if she were still here, I would have written this book. But this what the LORD has placed on my heart. To share with others what He has done and how He has helped me during this battle. There are some things you will never learn about God, until you are in the fiery furnace, and this is the whole purpose behind this book.

Since Angie went home, I have taken the opportunity that He has given me to separate myself from the world and dig even more into the Word of God. Not every trial that comes into our lives is from the LORD. What do I mean by that you may be asking? I thought He was in control of all things. Well, let me explain myself. What I am saying is, God is not the author of every trial. He allows every trial, but He is not the author. How do I know this? We learn in the book of Job that Satan has access to the Throne of God. We read in *Job 1:6-11; "Now there was a day when the sons of God came to present themselves before the LORD, and Satan also came among them. And the LORD said to Satan, "From where do you come?" So Satan answered the LORD and said, "From going to and fro on the earth, and from walking back and forth on it." Then the Lord said to Satan, "Have you considered My servant Job, that there is none like him on the earth, a blameless and upright man, one who fears God and shuns evil"; So Satan answered the LORD and said, "Does not Job fear God for nothing? Have You not made a hedge around him, around his household, and around all that he has on every side? You have blessed the work of his hands, and his possessions have increased in the land. But now, stretch out Your hand and touch all that he has, and he will surely curse You to Your face!"* We also learn in Job 1:12 that God sets the parameters of the attacks; *and the LORD said to Satan, "Behold, all that he has is in your power, only do not lay a hand on his person."* Satan then proceeds to kill all his children with a tornado or cyclone causing the house they were gathered in to collapse on top them, he has different bands of thieves steal all his herds and flocks, all just to get Job to curse God to His face. Then as if that was not enough, in *Job 2:4-7; "So Satan answered the LORD and said, "Skin for skin! Yes, all that a man has he will give for his life. But stretch out Your hand now, and touch his bone and his flesh, and he will surely curse You to Your face!" And the LORD said to Satan, "Behold, he is in your hand, but spare his life." So Satan went out from the presence of the LORD, and struck Job with painful boils from the sole of his foot to the crown of his head."*

If you are living a life that is surrendered to the LORD, the trials you are enduring are likely attacks from Satan. He wants to destroy all of humanity especially anyone who is living in obedience to the LORD. Remember what *I Peter 5:8 states; "Be sober, be vigilant; because your adversary the devil walks about like a roaring lion, seeking whom he may devour."* Satan wants us to get bitter and turn away from God. I did that earlier in my life, and I made a mess of it. And that is what he wants me to do now. As I said before, when we got the diagnosis on January 6th, I was angry at God for allowing this to happen, but I knew that the only place I could go to get the help I needed was to Him. And even though He did not heal Angie the way I wanted and was expecting, I am not about to turn away now. The understanding that I have gained in the past two years is priceless. I do not like the situation I currently find myself in by any stretch of the imagination. I miss my bride! But God does not promise a life free of trials and tribulations. In fact, He promises that we will have troubles. *John 16:33 says; "These things I have spoken to you, that in Me you may have peace. In the world you will have tribulation; but be of good cheer I have overcome the world."* Did you get that? He said we WILL have tribulation! But He also promises that we are not alone when we are going through the valley of testing. *Hebrews 13:5b-6* says, "For He Himself has said, "I will never leave you or forsake you," so we may boldly say: The LORD is my helper; I will not fear. What can man do to me?"

One thing that has really been a help to me during this time of testing, is gaining a better understanding of how the LORD sees me. One evening while I was working on this book, He spoke to my heart, "You are a pearl of great price." I was caught off guard by that. Since surrendering everyone and everything to the LORD in May of 2006, I have never considered myself a pearl of great price. Quite the contrary, I would continually struggle, seeing myself through my eyes not His. Through my eyes, all I ever saw was my failures. If you had the past that I have it would be hard to see yourself any other way. I struggled with legalism for a short time, because I was trying to earn or deserve His grace. This again, was because I could not see myself the way He does. So, when He spoke this to my heart, I had to go and read again the parable that the LORD taught in *Matthew 13:45-46; "Again, the kingdom of heaven is like a merchant seeking beautiful pearls, who when he had found one pearl of great price, went and sold all that he had and bought it."* I have always understood this parable as the merchant being a lost person without Christ, coming to Him for salvation and Christ is the pearl. But this is not the only interpretation.

We have some big misconceptions about God. Some think that He is distant, uninvolved and does not really care about us. Another misconception is that He is sitting on His throne waiting to nail us when we mess up. Well, these are just a few of the many lies from the enemy. God is involved in the affairs of humanity. *Proverbs 21:1 says, "The king's heart is in the hand of the LORD, like rivers of water; He turns it wherever He wishes.* He does care about mankind, *John 3:16-17; "For God so loved the world that He gave His only begotten Son, that whoever believes in Him should not perish but have everlasting life. For God did not send His Son into the world to condemn the world, but that the world through him might be saved." Psalm 145:8 says, "The Lord is gracious and full of compassion, slow to anger and great in mercy." II Peter 3:9 says, "The LORD is not slack concerning His promise, as some men count slackness, but is longsuffering toward us, not willing that any should perish, but that all would come to repentance."* These are just a few verses that you can use to counter the lies of the enemy. The whole Bible, both Old and New Testament, is God's love story to humanity! Do not let the enemy convince you that you are not loved! Just look to the Cross!

So, when I read the parable again, He spoke to my heart and said, "This is what I did for you." As I pondered on this, joy flooded my soul and tears started flowing and all I could do was worship. You see, Jesus paid it ALL for me! But the great thing about that is that it's not just me He sees that way! Everyone that has ever lived or ever will live is a pearl of great price in His eyes! Even those who have and who will reject His love. You may be asking why is this such a big deal? The answer is easy! I know the things I've done, the things I've said, the places I've been, the things I've seen, and I could go on. I am guilty of breaking all ten of the Ten Commandments, and not just in spirit, plus a bunch more. There is only one person who knows everything there is to know about me and that is Jesus. And He sees me as a pearl of great price! Think about that! I mean really! Let that thought sink in! He knows everything about everyone. Google only thinks they know everything. Ask yourself, have I ever had a lustful thought, or in a moment of anger, wish harm on someone else in your mind. You may think that you are the only one who knows, but the Bible says different. *Psalm 139:1-4(AMP) says; "O LORD you have searched me [thoroughly] and have known me. You know when I sit down and when I rise up [my entire life, everything I do]; You understand my thought from afar. You scrutinize my path and my lying down, and You are intimately acquainted with all my ways. Even before there is a word on my tongue [still unspoken], behold O LORD, You know it all. It goes on to say in verses 13-16; For You formed my innermost parts; You knit me [together] in my mother's womb. I will give thanks and praise to You, for I am fearfully and wonderfully made; wonderful are Your works; and my soul knows it very well. My frame was not hidden from you, when I was being formed in secret, and intricately and skillfully formed [as if embroidered with many colors] in the depths of the earth. Your eyes have seen my unformed substance; and in Your book were all written the days that were appointed for me, as yet there was not one of them [even taking shape]."*

Like I said everything! There is nothing hidden from Him! And to Him I am a pearl of great price. When you have the past that I have, that is saying something! I am not proud of my past, not in the least bit. But it is what it is, and there is nothing I can do to change it. The point I want you to get is this, it does not matter what you have done! You are a pearl of great price to the LORD! Like I said I am not proud of my past, but it has all been forgiven, never to be remembered again! *Hebrews 10:16-17 puts it this way; "This is the covenant I will make with them after those days says the LORD: I will put my laws in their hearts, and in their minds I will write them,"* then He adds, *"Their sins and their lawless deeds I will remember no more."* Did you get that! He chooses never to bring into His mind, not even one sin! Tell me that is not awesome! He is not like us! Even when we, with His help, forgive someone, whenever we see that person, or they come up in conversation, we remember the wrong that was done against us. Even though we have forgiven them, we still remember. We can make the choice to let that thought go through, or we can dwell on it. But God does not even let it enter His mind again! Once you have placed your trust in Jesus Christ, He justifies you and you are forgiven! He looks at you as if you have never committed a single sin! How AWESOME is that!

Now that doesn't mean you get to live however you want. No, quite the contrary. We as true followers of Jesus Christ are called to live in a way that brings honor and glory to our LORD. *Romans 12:1-2 states; "I beseech you therefore brethren, by the mercies of God, that you present your bodies a living sacrifice, holy, acceptable unto God, which is your reasonable service. And be not conformed to this world, but be transformed by the renewing of your mind, that you may prove what is that good and acceptable and perfect will of God."* The natural mind without the indwelling Holy Spirit is an enemy of God as stated in *Romans 8:7, "Because the carnal mind is enmity against God; for it is not subject to the law of God, nor indeed can be,"* and it does not have the capability of fully knowing the will of God, yet, once you place your trust in Christ, that changes! Praise His name! That is when the transformation starts! You are then sealed by the Holy Spirit. *Ephesians 4:30; "And do not grieve the Holy Spirit of God, by whom you were sealed for the day of redemption."* *Ephesians 1:13-14 also says; "In Him you also trusted, after you heard the word of truth, the gospel of your salvation; in whom also having believed, you were sealed with the Holy Spirit of promise, who is the guarantee of our inheritance until the redemption of the purchased possession, to the praise of His glory."* As we surrender our lives to the LORD, His Holy Spirit begins to open our eyes to see things from God's point of view. This process is called sanctification and it is a continual process. It will continue until either the LORD returns, or He calls you home as *Philippians 1:6 states, "being confident of this very thing, that He who has begun a good work in you will complete it until the day of Jesus Christ."*

Sanctification takes place at different rates for everyone. Speaking from personal experience, the sooner you surrender to His will, the sooner you will have the peace and joy the Bible teaches that is available to all believers. Take my advice and do not walk away from Him! No matter what He allows! Do not get bitter! Do not fight against Him! If you truly are a child of God, you cannot live outside His will and be at peace! I was, without a doubt, the most miserable when I was living as a prodigal! I knew I wasn't living in a way that pleased the LORD. But I refused to let go of the anger, bitterness, and unforgiveness that I had held onto for so long. Sometimes, for those of us that are too hardheaded for our own good, must be put in a position where we have nowhere else to turn. The

LORD will not force Himself on anyone and He will not help you until you come to Him. And that is where I found myself that afternoon in May of 2006, nowhere else to turn.

Since surrendering to Him, He has given me a greater understanding of His love for me. And with this understanding He has helped me see myself through His eyes. Being able to see myself through His eyes, makes me want to live right before Him. Because I now have a better understanding of what my sin cost Him. The Bible says in *Isaiah 53:5-6(AMP)*; *"But He was wounded for our transgressions, He was crushed for our wickedness [our sin, our injustice, our wrongdoing]; The punishment [required] for our well-being fell on Him, and by His stripes (wounds) we are healed. All of us like sheep have gone astray, we have turned, each one to his own way; but the LORD has caused the wickedness of us all [our sin, our injustice, our wrongdoing] to fall on Him [instead of us]."* When you truly get this understanding, you will never be the same! I do not want to do anything that would bring shame or reproach to the name of Christ! You may be asking, what about grace? Can I not live, and do however I want, because I have been forgiven? I'm glad you asked. The Bible says in *Romans 6:12-16; "Therefore do not let sin reign in your mortal body, that you should obey it in its lusts. And do not present your members as instruments of unrighteousness to sin, but present yourselves to God as being alive form the dead, and your members as instruments of righteousness to God. For sin shall not have dominion over you, for you are not under law but under grace. What then? Shall we sin because we are not under law but under grace? Certainly not! Do you not know that to whom you present yourselves to obey, you are that one's slaves whom you obey, whether of sin leading to death, or of obedience leading to righteousness?"* We all are serving someone! Who are you serving?

The Solution

We will be the only Bible that some people will ever see. As followers of Christ, we should strive to reflect our Savior. That does not, I repeat does not mean we will be perfect! But we should continue to grow. *II Corinthians 6:17a says; "Therefore come out from among them and be separate, says the LORD."* The desire of my heart is to be a light in my part of the world. Which is what the great commission is all about. *Mark 16:15-16; He said to them, "Go into all the world and preach the gospel to every creature. He who believes and is baptized will be saved; but he who does not will be condemned."*

One of the problems in this country today, is that we have too many people that name the name of Christ, but their lives do not look anything like His. Christians are not called to follow other Christians. We are called to follow Christ! We also are not to rely solely upon a preacher or some motivational speaker to tell us how to live. We are to take our instruction, with the help of the Holy Spirit, from the Word of God. *Joshua 1:8 says, "This book of the law shall not depart from your mouth, but you shall meditate in it day and night, that you may observe to do all that is written in it. For then you will make your way prosperous, and then you will have good success."* You may be thinking that is Old Testament law. We are living in the age of grace. I am glad you pointed that out. How about this? *II Timothy 3:16 states; "All scripture is given by inspiration of God, and is profitable for doctrine, for reproof, for correction, for instruction in righteousness."*

Another problem is that too many people do not slow down and take the time to let Him speak. When you don't take the time to be alone with God in prayer and reading His word, you start to drift and before you know it, you have lost direction and have no idea where you are heading. You lose your moral compass, you get desensitized, and you start to compromise your beliefs. I am speaking from experience, not passing judgement. It is easy to do. You must be intentional in your walk with Him. If you don't spend time alone with God, you will not have that close personal relationship that He so desires to have with you. It is relationship that you need to be the person He has called you to be. As followers of Christ, we have the greatest privilege in the world. We can come into the very presence of God any time of day or night. We do not need to call ahead and make an appointment and we are never told to come back later. We are told in *Hebrews 4:16; "Let us therefore come boldly to the throne of grace, that we may obtain mercy and find grace to help in time of need."* I am so thankful for this truth! I try every day to be more intentional in spending time with Him throughout the day, not just in my closet. Whether it's while I'm working, driving down the road, taking Leilu for a walk, or working out, I want Him to be a part of every area of my life. Let me give an example. One evening while I was waiting for our tub to fill up, I was in our bedroom listening to 106.9 The Light. It is a Christian radio station I listen to that was founded by the late Rev. Billy Graham. I happened to look down at the radio and saw a CD that a sweet lady, named Jill, gave me one Sunday at church. The title is *Hymns & Stories That are Important to Us*. It is by Joey and Rory Feek. There is a song that she wants me to listen to, called *When I'm Gone*. Joey had passed away after losing her battle with cancer. I have read the words, but I just have not been able to listen to the song yet. As I looked at the cover it reminded me of how anxious I am to see Angie again. While I was thinking about her, the Lord spoke to my heart, "As anxious as you are to be with her again, I am more anxious to be with you."

Whenever I think about heaven, I tend to think about all the blessings that await me. I do not believe I have ever considered or heard anyone preach about the fact that the Lord is anxiously waiting for me. *Hebrews 12:2 states, "looking unto Jesus, the author and finisher of our faith, who for the joy set before Him endured the cross, despising the shame, and has sat down at the right hand of the throne of God."* Who or what is the object of the joy that was set before Him? It was us! It was humanity!

We are the joy that was set before Him! Bringing us back into a right relationship with Himself was the reason He came! The Bible says only the Father knows the day of Jesus' return. *Mark 13:32 says; "But of that day and hour no one knows, not even the angels in heaven, nor the Son, but only the Father."* I remember after Angie and I set the date, the closer that day got the more anxious I became. The big difference is, I knew the date. He does not!

But He is seeing the prophesies come to pass, that He prophesied to His disciples before His ascension and those to John on the Isle of Patmos. He is seeing all the signs in the sun, the moon, and the stars. He knows that day is fast approaching. He just does not know when that day is. And in the meantime, He is interceding for His people and waiting for the Father to tell Him when He can go get His bride. I truly believe that day will happen during my life. With all the turmoil in our country and around the world and all the severe weather we have been having. Then, add to that, all the astronomical activity, such as the blood moons, that have been taking place. I cannot help but believe that that day is much closer than we think. Jesus tells His disciples in *Matthew 24:4-14; "Take heed that no one deceives you. For many will come in my name, saying I am the Christ and will deceive many. And you will hear of wars and rumors of wars. See that you are not troubled; for all these things must come to pass, but the end is not yet. For nation will rise against nation, and kingdom against kingdom. And there will be famines, pestilences, and earthquakes in various places. All these are the beginning of sorrows. Then they will deliver you up to tribulation and kill you, and you will be hated by all nations for my name's sake. And then many will be offended, will betray one another and hate one another. Then many false prophets will rise up and deceive many. And because lawlessness will abound, the love of many will grow cold. But he who endures to the end shall be saved. And this gospel of the kingdom will be preached in all the world as a witness to all nations and then the end will come."* I believe that day is fast approaching!

In my lifetime there has never been such a blatant disrespect for authority and the rule of law as we witness daily. What makes this even worse is that it's not just coming from the youth in this country. The youth are just imitating what they see from the "adults", and I use that term loosely, that are in positions of leadership. I have never seen a time when immorality is flaunted in the manner that it is today. As a nation we have forgotten how to blush. There is very little modesty in our country today. The sexualization of our society is in overdrive. And no matter how twisted your views are, you can find it on the internet. Nothing is left to the imagination. If you can think of it, you more than likely can find it.

You may be asking how did we get in this shape? That is a loaded question, with a complex answer. But I will keep it as simple as I can. The death of common sense is why we are in the shape we are in today. We have done away with our moral compass. A few people started complaining because they were offended by the Christian values and principles that were once proudly displayed in our public schools and other municipal buildings. Our leaders took it upon themselves and decided the best thing to do was to appease the minority, instead of standing with the majority of the US citizens. This allowed for the removal of prayer and the Ten Commandments from our public schools and other municipal buildings. It led to legalizing the murder of innocent babies and has led to all the mass shootings that have taken place in schools across the country.

When you remove the landmarks that our country was founded upon, this is what you get. Generation after generation falling further and further away from our Creator and losing the ability to discern the truth. When a lie is told loud enough long enough it becomes true, even though it is still factually a lie. What many people do not understand, is that there is a spiritual battle taking place. It is real! It doesn't matter if you believe it or not! *Ephesians 6:12-13 says, "For we do not wrestle against flesh and blood, but against principalities, against powers, against the rulers of the darkness of this age, against spiritual hosts of wickedness in the heavenly places. Therefore take up the whole armor of God, that you may be able to withstand in the evil day, and having done all, to stand."* This battle goes back before the Garden of Eden. A time when Lucifer, an archangel created by God, looked to unseat God as the Supreme being in the Universe. The Bible tells us in *Isaiah 14:12-15; "how you are fallen from heaven, O Lucifer, son of the morning! How you are cut down to the ground. You who weakened the nations! For you have said in your heart: I will ascend into heaven, I will exalt my throne above the stars of God; I will also sit on the mount of the congregation on the furthest side of the north; I will ascend above the heights of the clouds, I will be like the Most High: yet you shall be brought down to Sheol, to the lowest depths of the Pit. "* For his rebellious pride, Lucifer lost his position and name. He also led one third of the angels with him in his rebellion.

People have tried to argue that the US was not founded on Christian principles, yet on November 11, 1620, The Mayflower Compact was signed by forty-one men, who had spent more than two months at sea, before anchoring of Cape Cod. These men were part of a group of people who left Europe for multiple reasons. One of those reasons was for the spread of the Gospel of our Lord and Savior Jesus Christ. These men made their faith known in the first few lines of this historic document; "In the name of God, Amen. We, whose names are underwritten, the loyal subjects of our dread sovereign lord, King James, by the grace of God, of England, France, and Ireland, Defender of the Faith. Having undertaken for the glory of God, and advancement of the Christian Faith, and honour of our King and country, a voyage to plant the first colony in the northern parts of Virginia." This is where it began for the US! Common sense was born in the new world. The seed of Christianity was planted, and like it always does when it is planted in fertile soil, it grew from there. People can keep trying to rewrite history all they want. But the facts are the facts. You cannot dispute that! It is there plain as day in black and white. From that point on America has been and continues to be a Christian nation. Like it or not it is what is and there is nothing no one can do to change that.

According to a post on newsmax.com written by Scott Rasmussen on March 30, 2018, 71% of Americans identify as Christian. He goes on further to break them down into five separate groups: 25% Evangelical, 20% Catholic, 15% mainline Protestant, 7% attending historically black Protestant churches, and the remaining 4% Mormon, Jehovah's Witness, other combined. Christianity has been on a steady decline for years. There are many reasons for that, but that is for another book. But the last time I checked 71% is greater than 50%. I will repeat what I said earlier. We have too many Christians following other Christians, instead of following Jesus. How else can you explain why we are in the shape we are as a nation. Think about it, if 71% of the people in this country were truly following the example the Lord that we claim to love gave us to follow, do you honestly believe we would be in the mess we are today? Do you think that the suicide rates of our youth would be climbing? What about abortion? How about the divorce rate? The answer to all is no! If 71% of the people in this country were truly following Jesus, there is no way this country would be this confused and messed up in the head.

Again, too many Christians rely wholly on what they hear from a preacher. They are trusting fully in this man's interpretation of God's word. They're too busy to take the time to invest personally in their relationship with the Lord. Far too many want the easy way out. They do not want to put in the work it takes build that close personal relationship. Let me ask you this question, "Do you have to work at your relationship with your spouse?" If you want a good relationship you do! What makes you think that it is any different in a relationship with the LORD? If you do not take time with Him, you will never know Him in the way He wants you to know Him. How can I say those things? Because that is where I was. I do not want you to misunderstand what I am saying, since May of

2006, I have tried to live a surrendered life. But it's easy to get caught up in day to day living and say I will read tomorrow, or I will pray tomorrow. Before you know it, the week is gone, and you haven't touched your Bible and you have only spoken to the LORD in passing moments throughout the week. To better know God, you must be intentional in your walk with Him. *Jeremiah 29:12-14a says; "Then you will call upon me and go and pray to me, and I will listen to you. And you will seek Me and find Me, when you search for Me with all your heart. I will be found by you says the Lord, and I will bring you back from your captivity."* When we do not take the time with our Creator, we become captives to our routines and schedules. God wants us to be free and filled with His Holy Spirit.

With all that Angie and I had been through and the fact that I had walked away before, I made it a point to take those verses in Jeremiah to heart when she was first diagnosed. I became more intentional in making time for Him, to pray, to read His word, and to listen for Him to speak. He promises in *James 4:8; "Draw near to God and He will draw near to you. Cleanse your hands, you sinners; and purify your hearts, you doubleminded."* And as He always is, He was faithful to that promise! I know Him better today than at any other time in my walk with Him. What this country and the world need to see are men and women seeking God with all their hearts, living in surrender to His will, instead of living for themselves and walking in disobedience. They need to see us love one another. *John 13:31 says; "By this all will know that you are my disciples, if you have love for one another."* In my opinion, John chapter 17 is one of, if not the greatest prayers in the Bible. Jesus is praying for Himself, His disciples, and for all present and future believers. *John 17:20-21 says, "I do not pray for these alone, but also for those who will believe in Me through their word; that they all may be one, as You, Father are in Me, and I in You; that they may also be one in us, that the world may believe that You sent Me."*

I know I am going to make some people mad by what I am about to say, but that is going to be ok! Denominations were not God's doing. They were man's doing. In *II Timothy 2:15, Paul tells a young preacher named Timothy to; "Be diligent to present yourself approved of God, a worker who does not need to be ashamed, rightly dividing the word of truth."* In other words what Paul is telling Timothy, is to be sure of what is being communicated. Know what God is saying in His word. He goes on to say in verses *16-18a; "But shun profane and idle babblings, for they will increase to more ungodliness. And their message will spread like cancer. Hymenaeus and Philetus are of this sort, who have strayed from the truth."* What has happened over time is, the misinterpretation of the Word of God has led to different denominations of what God intended to be One Faith and One Message. It is no wonder those who are spiritually blind, do not want anything to do with Christianity. They see that we the church cannot agree. They see all the infighting and that our lifestyles are not much different from theirs. So, why would they want to be a part of the mess that we have made of God's plan to save mankind?

Here is where I will make some of you mad. There is not going to be any Baptists, of which denomination I belong, in heaven! There is not going to be any Catholics in heaven! There is not going to be any Muslims in heaven! I don't care what religion or denomination you can come up with! The only people who are going to be in heaven are the true followers of Jesus Christ. When you stand before God, and you will, He is not going to care about anything other than what you did with Jesus! THAT'S IT! NOTHING ELSE WILL MATTER! And if you say no to His invitation, you will not have a place. *John 14:1-6 says, "Let not your heart be troubled; you believe in God, believe also in Me. In my Father's house are many mansions; if it were not so I would have told you. I go to prepare a place for you. And if I go to prepare a place for you, I will come again and receive you to myself; that where I am, you may be also. And Where I go you know, and the way you know." Thomas said to Him, "LORD, we do not know where You are going, and how can we know the* way?" Jesus said to him, "I am the way, the truth, and the life. No one comes to the Father except through me." There you have it! His words not mine. Know Jesus, know heaven! No Jesus, No heaven! There is only one way! This is not my opinion, and your unbelief will not change God's plan! It's His plan not yours! He is God! You are not! The Bible tells us in *Psalm 19:1-3; "The heavens declare the glory of God; and the firmament shows His handiwork. Day unto day utters speech, and night unto night reveals knowledge. There is no speech nor language where their voice is not heard!"* All you need to do is look up into the clear night sky! He has made it obvious! This did not happen by some cosmic accident! And the One who made it all has declared the way of salvation!

I had been feeling a bit overwhelmed but couldn't pinpoint a specific reason. It was more of a combination of things, that brought on these feelings. Angie's birthday had just passed. Her mom has not been in good health lately. There is strife in my family between my sister's family, and myself and our parents. And I have been frustrated with the media and all the garbage that is going on in the political arena. So, I was getting ready for a workout. I usually pray before a workout, and while I was praying, I asked the LORD to help me with how I was feeling. I had anger issues in my past, and I do not ever want to go back there. It is only by His grace and mercy that

I am not there now. I did my warmups and got ready for my workout. But I just didn't have it in me to work out. I usually just push through these times, but it was like the LORD was saying be still and worship. I realized that it had been a while since I had done that very thing. We do not just worship God in a church! We worship Him in Spirit and in Truth and that can take place pretty much anywhere and anytime. I went and ran a bath, I put my Selah CD You Amaze Us in the CD player, cranked it up and just meditated on the words of the first 6-8 songs. Talk about a much-needed help! If you have never just sat and listened to these songs, I strongly recommend taking the time to do so. You do not have to do the whole bath thing if you do not want to, I just have a thing for water. I love the water. I always have.

So, I am listening intently to these songs that glorify God, the Creator and Source of all life. I was thinking on the Greatness of our God and the arrogance and sheer audacity of man. In my opinion, those who believe in anything other than creation fall into this category. Why do people think that the laws of nature do not apply to the origin of the Universe? Death is the absence of life. Nothing living will ever come from death without the help of an external source. You can choose to believe it or not, but to put it in southern terms, "it ain't happening!" Think about it logically. I'm not even using the fact that the Bible gives us a detailed account. Take a car battery for example. When that battery is dead, you are not going anywhere. You can turn the switch as many times as you want to, but it is not going to crank the car. You have two options; replace the battery or try to charge it. There is no in between. The only way to put life back into that battery is with an electrical charge from an outside source. How about this for another example, if someone's heart stops and they die. It takes an outside force to bring them back. These are couple of examples of a law that cannot be broken. For life to exist as it does today, there must have been someone or some force outside space and time as we know it, that brought it to pass. Life can never come from death own its own period!

One of the reasons people believe the lies, is because we have been told to trust individuals with high IQs and all kinds of credentials after their names which supposedly makes them "experts" in that field. We are taught from a young age to trust and not to question those deemed smarter because they understand the "science". I have no doubt that these people are smart, but they have no common sense and denounce the obvious. They want to completely remove God from the equation. Just because someone has a high IQ does not mean they have wisdom or common sense. The Bible speaks of these people in *Romans 1:18-22; "For the wrath of God is revealed from Heaven against all ungodliness and unrighteousness of men, who suppress the truth in unrighteousness, because what may be known of God is manifest in them, for God has shown it to them. For since the creation of the world His invisible attributes are clearly seen, being understood by the things that are made, even His eternal power and Godhead, so that they are without excuse, because, although they knew God, they did not glorify Him as God, nor were thankful, but became futile in their thoughts, and their foolish hearts were darkened. Professing to be wise, they became fools." Psalm 53:1 emphatically states; "The fool has said in his heart, "There is no God." They are corrupt and have done abominable iniquity; There is none who does good."*

It used to amaze me that so many people believed any of the theories other than creation, given the amount of evidence that not only substantiates the belief in, but the claim of a Supreme Creator, by the three major religions of the world, Christianity, Judaism, and Islam. But when you are taught theories as truth without any counter belief, they become truth to those who have never been taught any different. And yet they're still only theories. They are other men's "scientific" opinions! There is not a solitary one that can be proven! Yet when given a detailed description of creation, with more evidence to back up the claims made, these same people scoff at the idea of a Creator. *Genesis 1:1 plainly states; "In the beginning*

God created the heavens and the earth." Then it goes on to give a detailed account of how and what He created. But many simply refuse to believe, and that is what is so sad! *Proverbs 14:6 states;* *"A scoffer seeks wisdom and does not find it, but knowledge is easy to him who understands."* These people are tools of the enemy, to bring about confusion. The Bible tells us in *I Corinthians 14:33; "For God is not the author of confusion but of peace."* It also says in *I Corinthians 3:19; "For the wisdom of this world is foolishness with God. For it is written, "He catches the wise in their craftiness."* There is coming a day when we all will stand before our Creator. Your unbelief will not change that! *Hebrews 9:27 says; "it is appointed for men to die once, but after this the judgment."* We are also told in *Philippians 2:10; "that at the name of Jesus every knee should bow, of those in heaven, and of those on earth, and of those under the earth, and that every tongue should confess that Jesus Christ is LORD, to the glory of God the Father."*

You can either bow now in humble adoration, or you will bow trembling in FEAR and AWE at His return. One way or the other we will all bow before the Sovereign Creator of ALL things! He leaves the choice up to us. He gives us the choice, because without a choice it is not love but slavery. He does not want slaves! He wants your love! He wants you to willingly choose Him and eternal life! That is why He sent Jesus! He wants you to be with Him for all eternity! God does not send anyone to hell! They willingly choose to go there! Anyone that goes to hell, goes as an intruder, because God created hell for the devil and all the angels that rebelled with him, not people! *Proverbs 14:12 says; "there is a way that seems right to a man, but its end is death."* I cannot stress this enough! Your unbelief will not change one thing about God's word. But if you place your faith in Jesus Christ, you get your name written in the Lamb's Book of Life!

Let me tell you why that is SO IMPORTANT! *Revelation 20:11-15 says, "Then I saw a great white throne and Him who sat on it, from whose face the earth and heaven fled away. And there was found no place for them. And I saw the dead, small and great, standing before God, and books were opened. And another book was opened, which is the Book of Life. And the dead were judged according to their works, by the things which were written in the books. The sea gave up the dead who were in it, and Death and Hades delivered up the dead who were in them. And they were judged, each one according to his works. Then Death and Hades were cast into the lake of fire. This is the second death. And anyone not found written in the Book of Life was cast into the lake of fire."* You will spend eternity in one of two places and the choice is all up to you!

I am so thankful that my name is written in the Book of

Life! I have a hope that can never be taken from me. There is a better day ahead for the child of God. And contrary to popular belief we are not all God's children! Do not take my word for it. Look it up for yourself. *John 1:10-13 says, "He was in the world, and the world was made through Him, and the world did not know Him. He came to His own, and His own did not receive Him. But as many as received Him, to them He gave the right to be children of God, to those who believe in His name: who were born, not of blood, nor of the will of the flesh, nor of the will of man, but of God."* If you want to see heaven, you must go by way of the Cross. There is no other way to get your name in the Book of Life! Because my name is written down, I will see Angie, Bailey, Matthew, Terry, Jimmy, my papaw Poole, and many more that have gone on before me. It is not because we are good that we get to go to heaven. It is because He is! We are incapable of being good enough! If we could, then Jesus would have never gone to the cross.

There are not multiple roads to heaven! There is only One! In *Matthew 7:13-14 the Lord says, "Enter by the narrow gate; for wide is the gate and broad is the way that leads to destruction, and there be many who go in by it. Because narrow is the gate and difficult is the way which leads to life, and there are few who find it."* These are not my words. They are the words of Jesus Christ! He also warns us in *Mark 13:22, "For false christs and false prophets will rise and show signs and wonders to deceive, if possible, even the elect."* He is speaking of others who say there is another way to heaven other than through Him. John warns about false doctrine in *Revelation 22:18-19; "For I testify to everyone who hears the words of the prophecy of this book: If anyone adds to these things, God will add to him the plagues that are written in this book; and if anyone takes away from the words of the book of this prophecy, God shall take away his part from the Book of Life, from the holy city, and from the things which are written in this book."* This choice is yours and yours alone! No one else can make it for you! It all boils down to what you are going to choose to believe.

We all must choose to believe something! Will you believe the truth, or one of many lies? *John 17:17 says; "Sanctify them by Your truth. Your word is truth."* Did you get that? There is an absolute truth! The Bible is the Word of the Living God! All it takes is a little faith and a little common sense! *Acts 1:1-3 says; "The former account I made, O Theophilus, of all that Jesus began both to do and teach, until the day in which He was taken up, after He through the Holy Spirit had given commandments to the apostles whom He had chosen, to whom He also presented Himself alive after His suffering by many infallible proofs, being seen forty days and speaking of the things pertaining to the kingdom of God."* Then go to *I Corinthians 15:3-8, where Paul gives his account;*

"For I delivered to you first of all that which I also received: that Christ died for our sins according to the Scriptures, and that He was buried, and that He rose again the third day according to the Scriptures, and that He was seen by Cephas, then the twelve. After that He was seen by James, then by all the apostles. Then last of all He was seen by me also, as by one born out of due time."

Here is where the common sense comes in. I really want you to think about the question I am about to ask! I want you to put yourself in the position of these apostles. Would you die for a deliberate lie? Would you be willing to be tortured for something that you knew without a doubt was a lie? All the apostles were martyred for their faith in Christ, except for John, who spent the remainder of his life in forced isolation on the Isle of Patmos. These were not hardened soldiers. They were common men of the day, fishermen, tax collectors, etc. If Jesus is dead, these men were either the dumbest men in history or the some of the evilest, you decide. Ask yourself these questions: Would I let myself be burned alive for a lie? Would I let myself be beaten with a cat of nine tails, a Roman whip used to beat Jesus, for a lie? Would I let myself be crucified upside down for a lie? Would I let myself be eaten alive by lions, for a lie? The Romans were cruel in their torture tactics. They wanted to inflict as much pain as possible before they let you die. So, again, I ask you, would you allow any of these things happen to you or someone you love for a lie that you knew was a lie? I know I wouldn't, and my guess is that you wouldn't either. So, why do people think that these common, ordinary men would? The greatest testimony that Jesus Christ is alive is Christianity itself.

If you want to be sure of an eternity of peace and joy all you need to do is place your faith in the death, burial, and resurrection of Jesus Christ. *Romans 10:13 says; "For whoever calls on the LORD shall be saved."* If you are asking, Shannon how do I call upon the name of the LORD? The answer is found in *Romans 10:9-10; "that if you confess with your mouth the LORD Jesus and believe in your heart that God has raised Him from the dead, you will be saved. For with the heart one believes unto righteousness, and with the mouth confession is made unto salvation."* God made salvation easy! And by the way it is His plan! Who are we to tell Him how it should be! He says there is but one way, and that way is through Jesus. The great news about that is this, it is for everyone! There are no exclusions! Again, *John 3:16-17; "For God so loved the world that He gave His only begotten Son, that whoever believes in Him will not perish but have everlasting life. For God did not send His Son into the world to condemn the world, but that the world through Him might be saved."* Now, I want you to put your name every place where the word world is. He came for you, for me, and for every person that has ever lived or ever will live. This hope can be yours! If you have felt the LORD tugging at your heart while reading this book, I hope and pray that you will ask Him to save you. It is that simple! All you need to do is ask! *John 6:37 says; "All that the Father gives Me will come to Me, and he who comes to Me I will by no means cast out."* That is an iron clad promise!

Just pray, Dear God, I believe your word and that I am a sinner. I believe that Your Son, Jesus Christ, died on the cross to pay for my sins. I believe that He arose on the third day and that He is alive and is coming again. Dear LORD, I ask you to forgive me of my sins and to come into my heart and save me now. Thank you, Father for saving me and sealing me with Your Holy Spirit, in Jesus' name, Amen. If you prayed that prayer and meant it with all your heart, you are now a child of the Living God! You now have a hope and a future that no one can take from you! If we never meet on this side of heaven, please come, and find me when we get there. I look forward to meeting you in that Beautiful City! *"He who testifies to these things says, "Surely I am coming quickly." Amen. Even so, come, Lord Jesus!" Revelation 22:20.*